Coloring Book

ANIMALS
of
AUSTRALIA

Mark Shawe

Book Series: Animal Planet

In this Coloring Book you will find:

- 20 original realistic full-page images of wild animals of Australia on single-sided sheets to prevent bleed-through
- 60 interesting unusual facts about the animals

Grab you favorite tool: pencils, crayons, markers or paints, and start coloring!

ISBN: 9781079226393

WORLD MAP

Koala

It is thought that koala means 'no drink' in some ancient aboriginal languages. Like humans, koalas have fingerprints. While there are more than 600 varieties of Eucalyptus trees available in the koala's habitat, the animal really loves to eat roughly 30-40 of these species. Eucalyptus is poisonous to most animals. The koala's digestive system creates bacteria that deactivate the poison. The Eucalyptus tree is not protected and as more of these trees are cut down, the numbers of koalas are reduced.

life expectancy in nature

16

0   25   50   75   100

weigh up to   6 kg (13 lb)

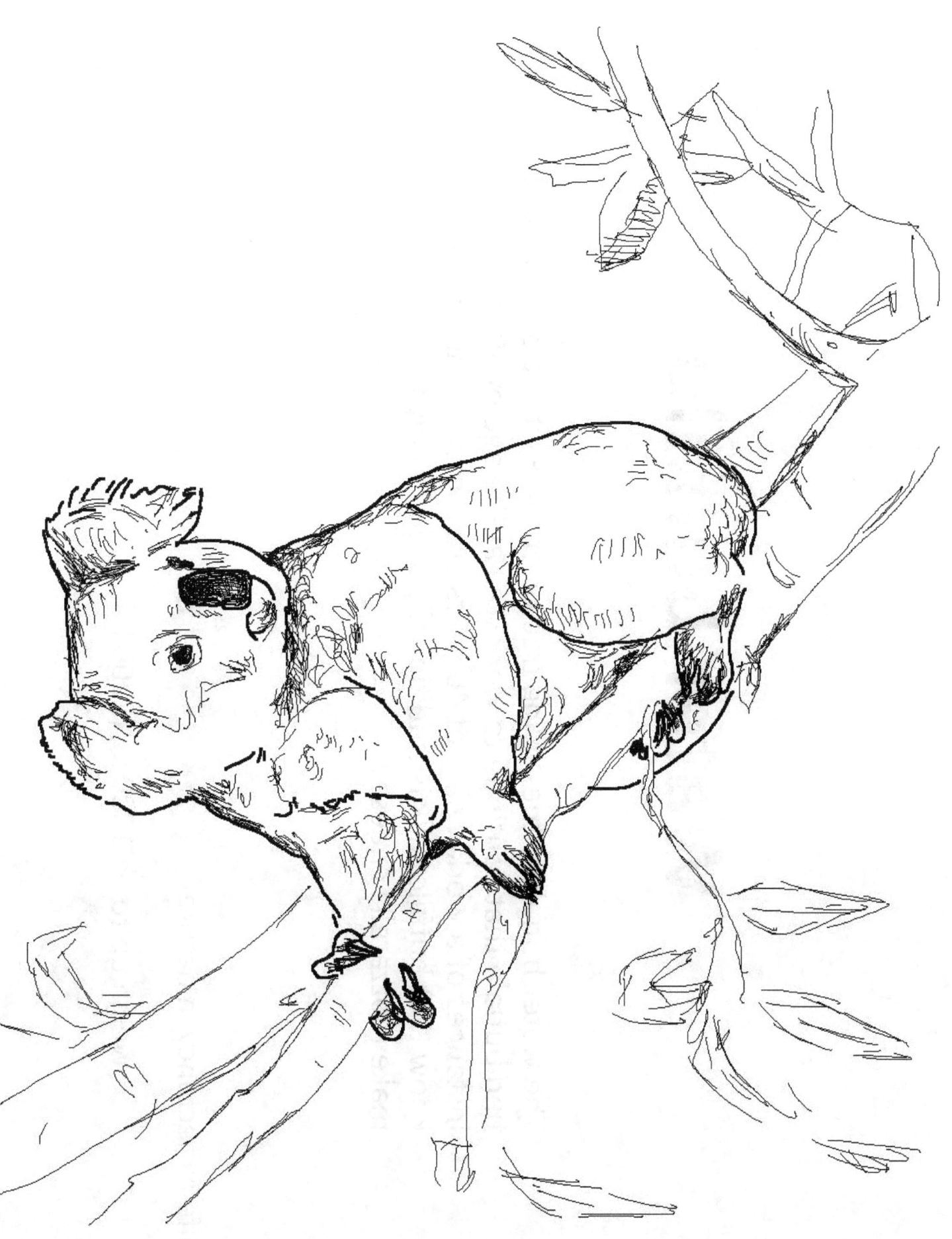

Water buffalo

The water buffalo is the "living tractor of the East." It is not rare to find buffalo that continue to work well at the age of 30, and instances of a working life of 40 years are recorded. And did you know that buffalo milk is traditionally used in Italy to make mozzarella cheese?

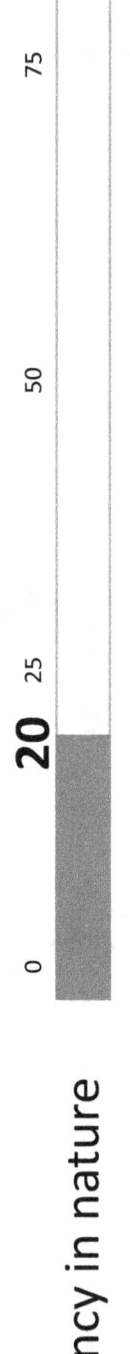

life expectancy in nature

0   20   25   50   75   100

weigh up to   1000 kg (2200 lb)

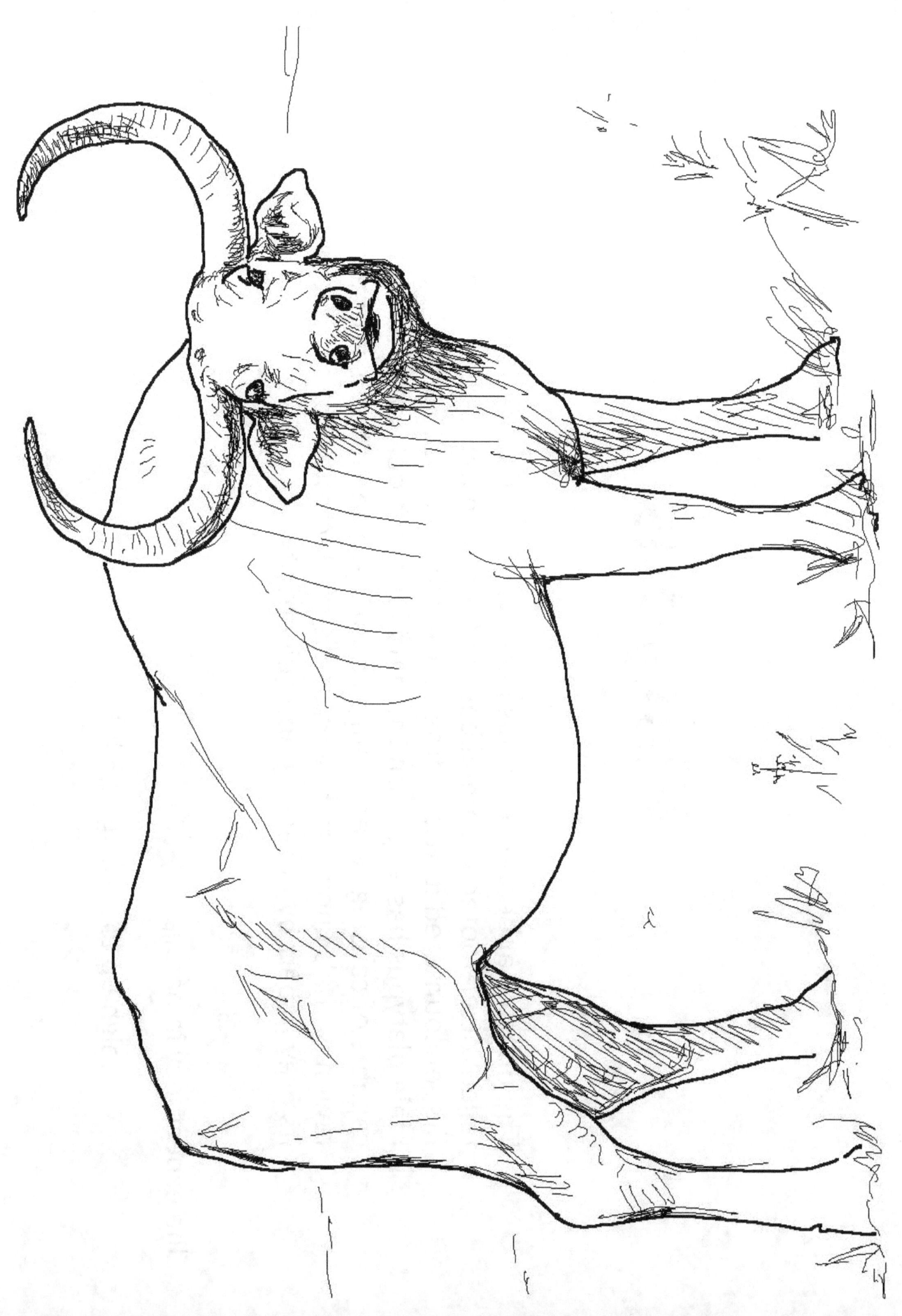

Platypus

The unusual appearance of this egg-laying, duck-billed, beaver-tailed, otter-footed mammal baffled European naturalists when they first encountered it, with some considering it an elaborate hoax. The male platypus has a spur on the hind foot that delivers a venom capable of causing severe pain to humans. The Platypus is one of the few mammals known to have a sense of electroreception: it locates its prey in part by detecting body electricity.

life expectancy in nature

| 0 | **10** | 25 | 50 | 75 | 100 |

weigh up to   2 kg (4,5 lb)

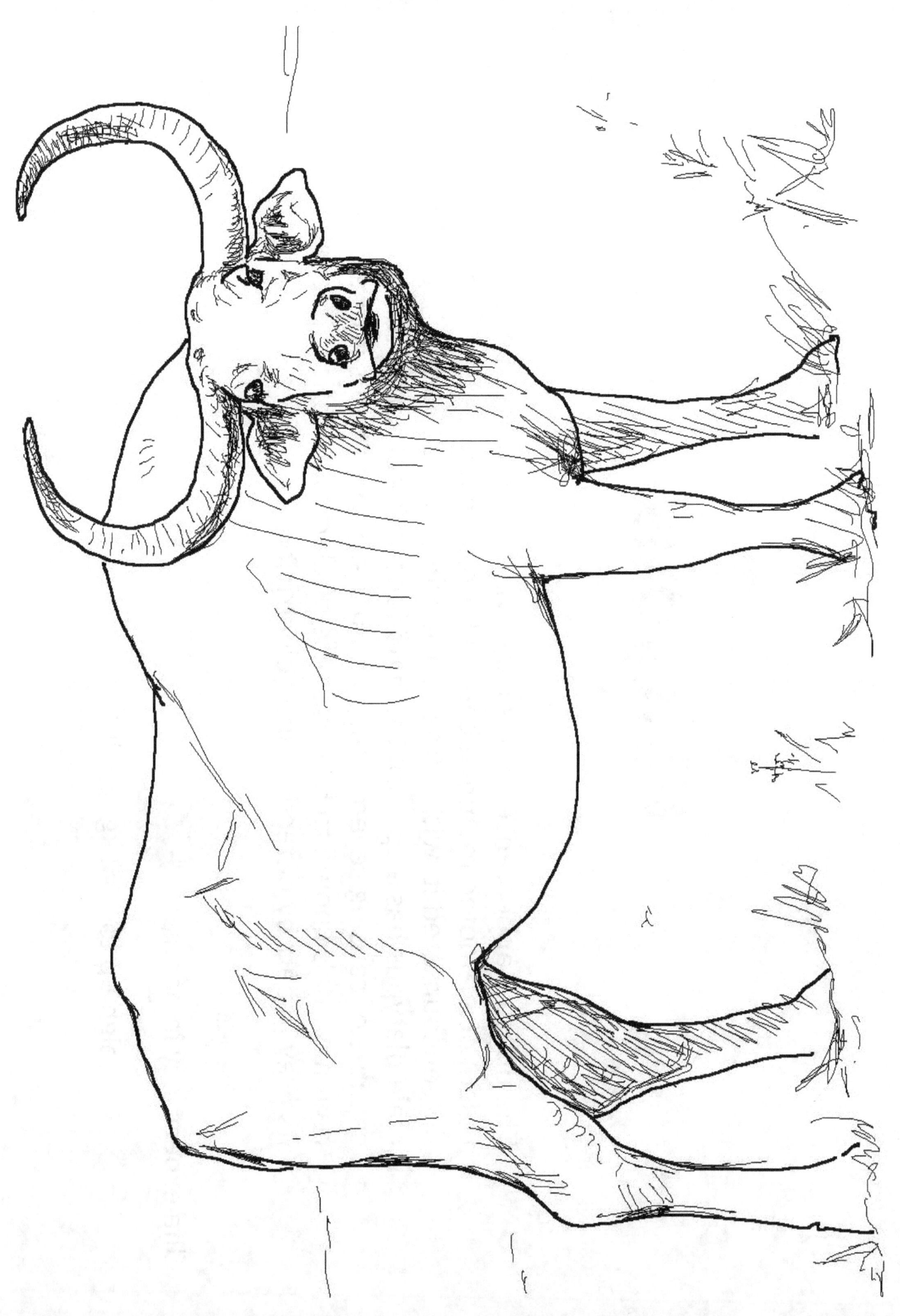

Platypus

The unusual appearance of this egg-laying, duck-billed, beaver-tailed, otter-footed mammal baffled European naturalists when they first encountered it, with some considering it an elaborate hoax. The male platypus has a spur on the hind foot that delivers a venom capable of causing severe pain to humans. The Platypus is one of the few mammals known to have a sense of electroreception: it locates its prey in part by detecting body electricity.

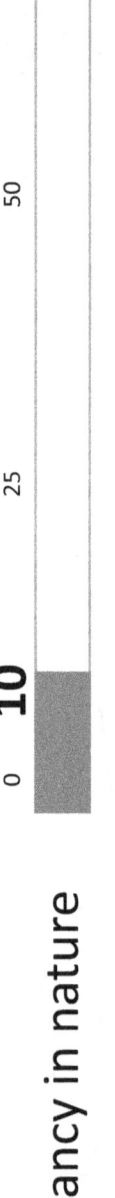

life expectancy in nature

weigh up to   2 kg (4,5 lb)

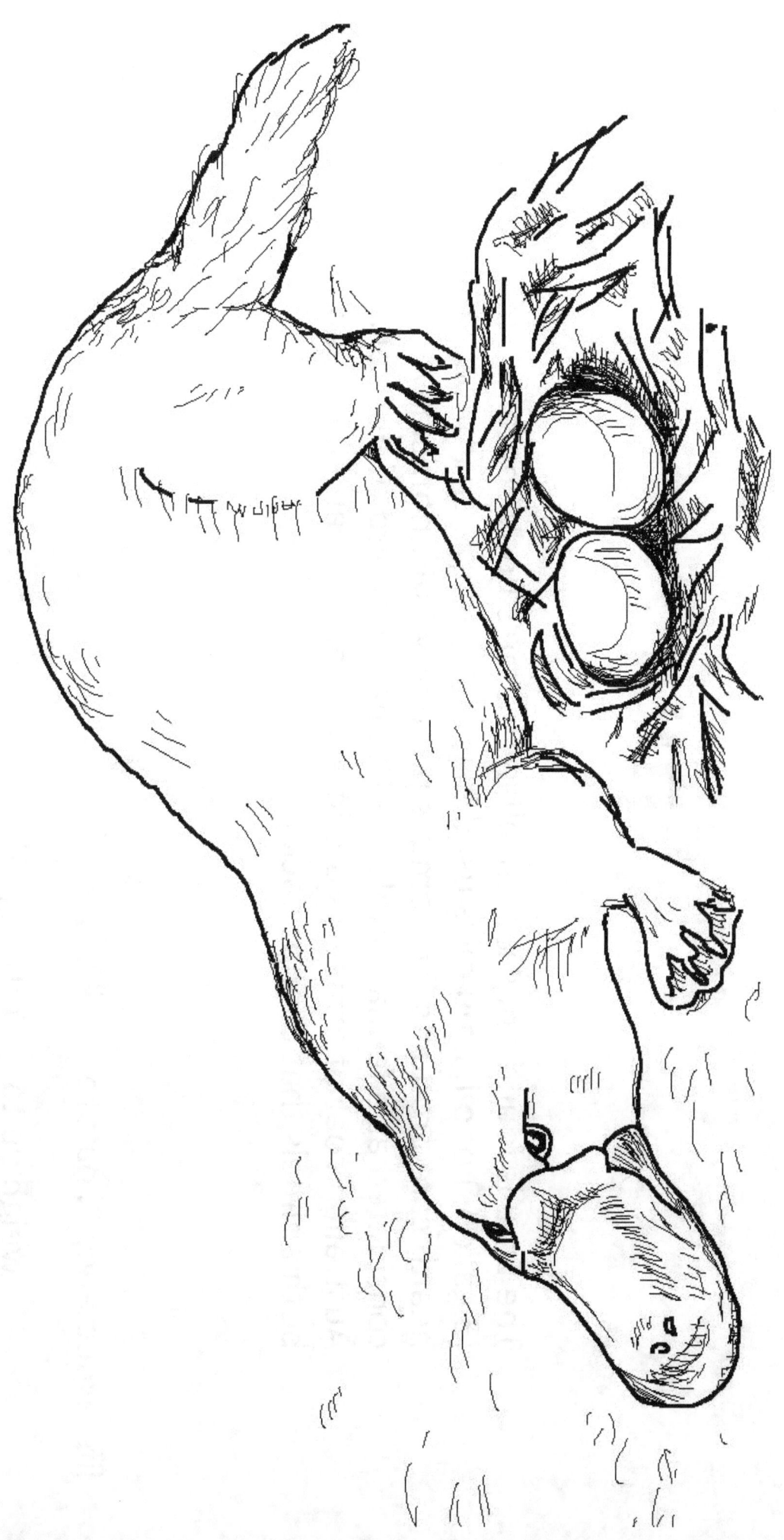

Emu

The Emu is found only in Australia. An emu's body contains 13.5 liters (3 gallons) of oil. Emu oil is used in lotions, soaps, shampoo, and health care products. The emu is popularly but unofficially considered as a faunal emblem – the national bird of Australia. The Australian coat of arms has the image of an emu and a kangaroo, both animals that cannot back up

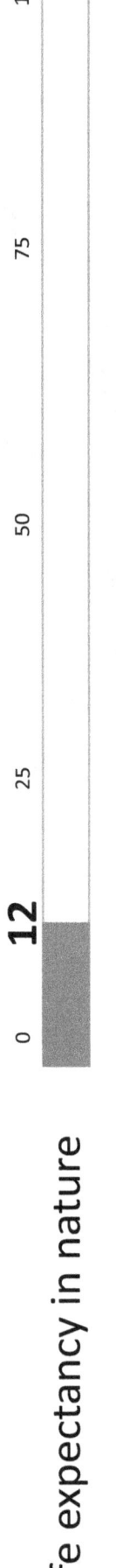

life expectancy in nature

weigh up to   160 kg (350 lb)

0   **12**   25   50   75   100

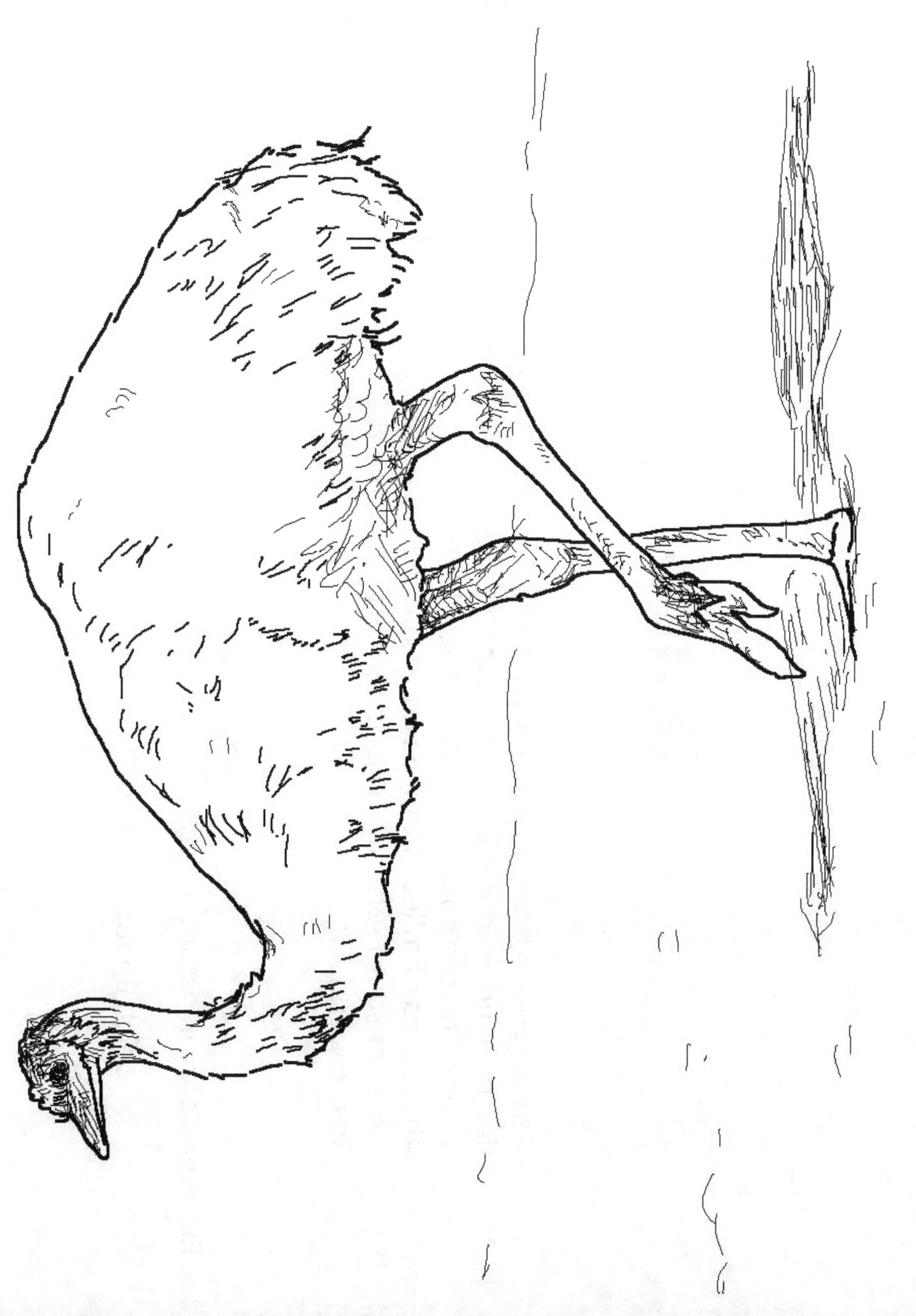

Dingo

The dingo is a type of feral dog native to Australia. They are the largest land predator in Australia. In the 1920s, the Dingo Fence was erected on the basis of the Wild Dog Act (1921) and, until 1931, thousands of miles of Dingo Fences had been erected in several areas of South Australia. It is generally considered the longest fence in the world.

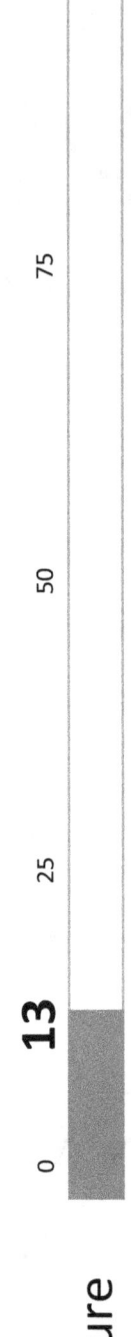

life expectancy in nature

0   **13**   25   50   75   100

weigh up to   19 kg (42 lb)

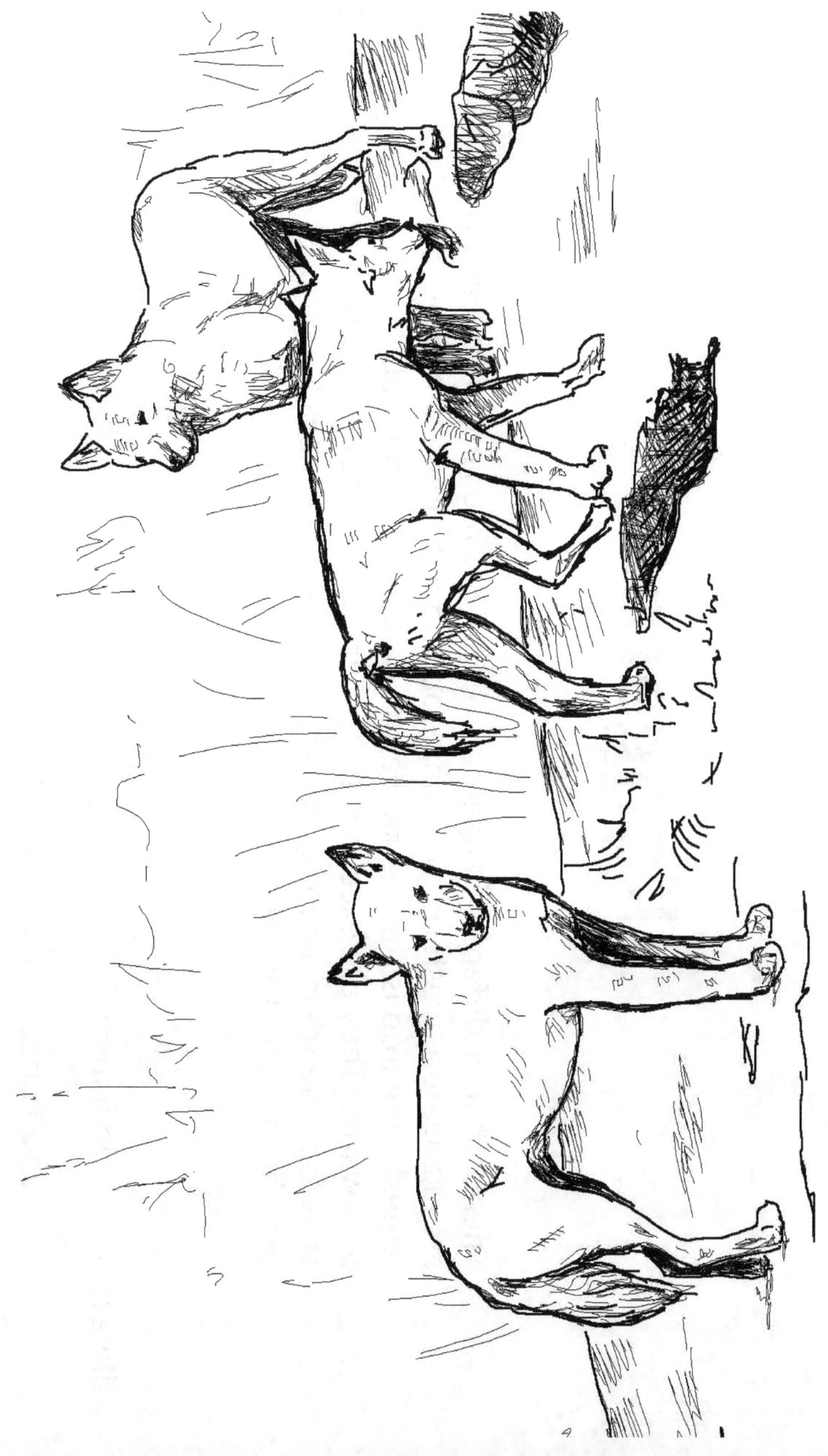

Kangaroo

There are four different kangaroo species, the red kangaroo, eastern grey kangaroo, western grey kangaroo and antilopine kangaroo. The largest kangaroo is the red kangaroo. Kangaroos can't walk backwards. They are excellent swimmers. When they swim, they are able to move their hind legs separately. There are more kangaroos than humans in Australia.

life expectancy in nature

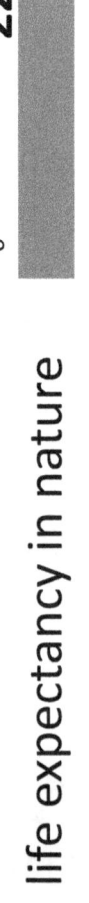

22

0   25   50   75   100

weigh up to   85 kg (188 lb)

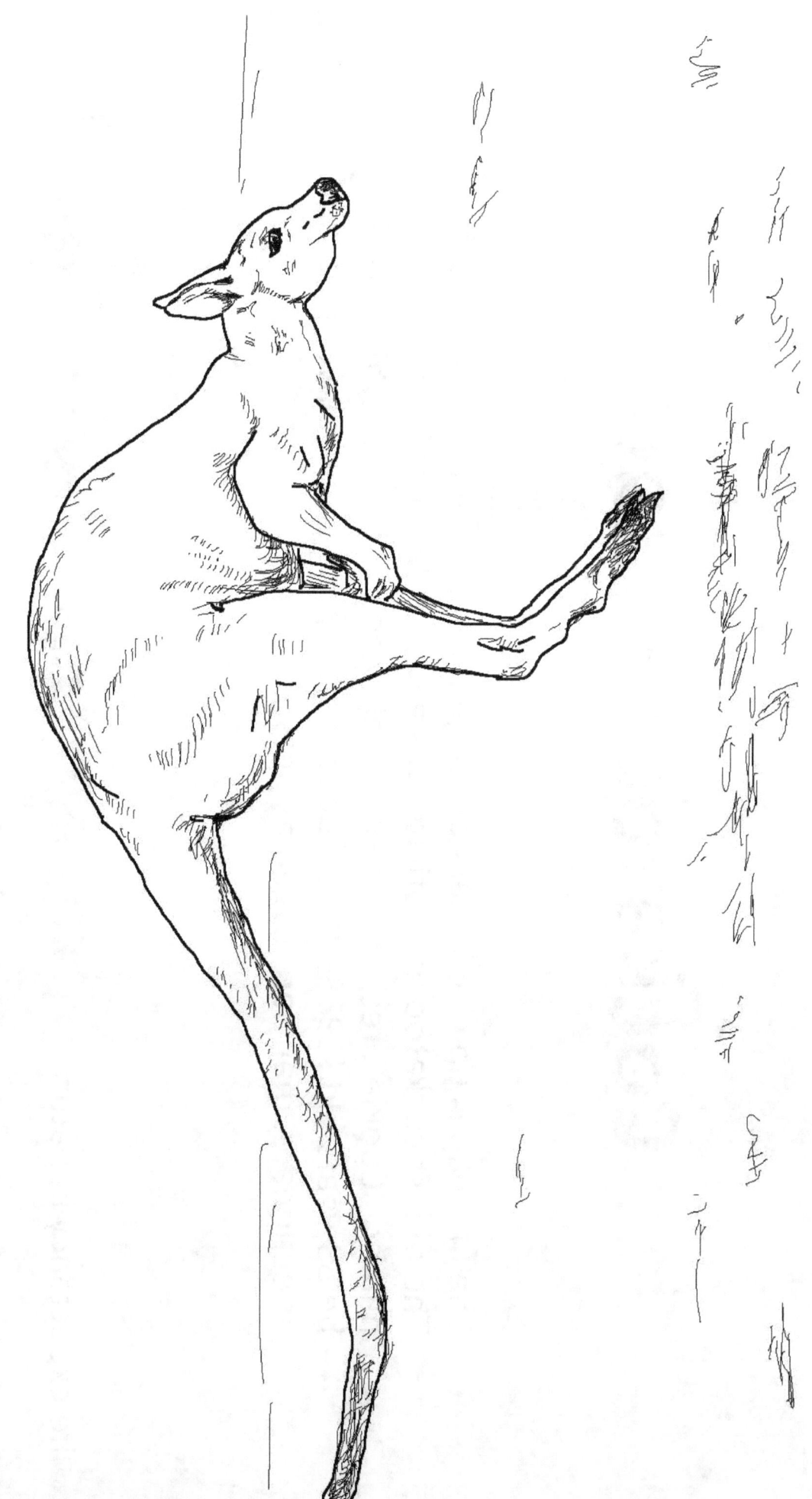

Cockatoo Kakadu

The lifespan is up to 60 years or longer, depending upon the species. The oldest cockatoo in captivity was a Major Mitchell's cockatoo named "Cookie", residing at Brookfield Zoo in Chicago, which lived to be 83 years old (1933–2016). Because they are showy, inventive, and affectionate, many are caged as pets.

life expectancy in nature

| 0 | 25 | 50 | 75 | **90** | 100 |

weigh up to   0,9 kg (1,98 lb)

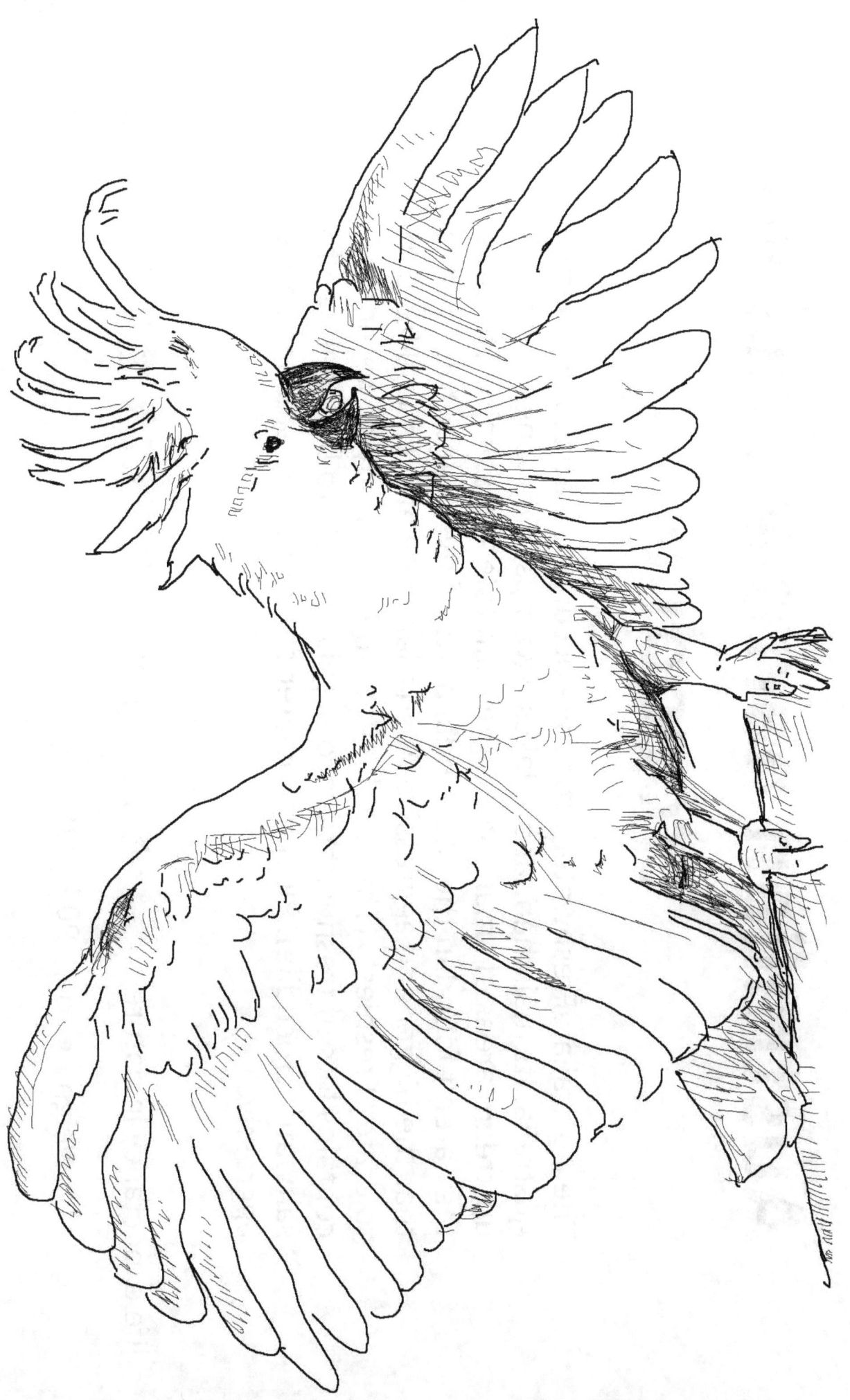

Australian narrow-necked crocodile

The Australian Freshwater Crocodile occurs only across northern Australia. Its main habitat are lakes, swamps, billabongs and the upstream areas of small rivers. They can tolerate salinity. The reason they aren't found in the more tidal parts of rivers near the coast is that the bigger and aggressive Australian saltwater crocodiles don't tolerate "Freshies". (That can be good news. A body of water that contains lots of freshwater crocodiles is unlikely to be inhabited by a saltwater crocodile). Plus, freshwater crocodiles are smaller and less aggressive.

life expectancy in nature

| 0 | 25 | 50 | 75 | **95** | 100 |

weigh up to   90 kg (198 lb)

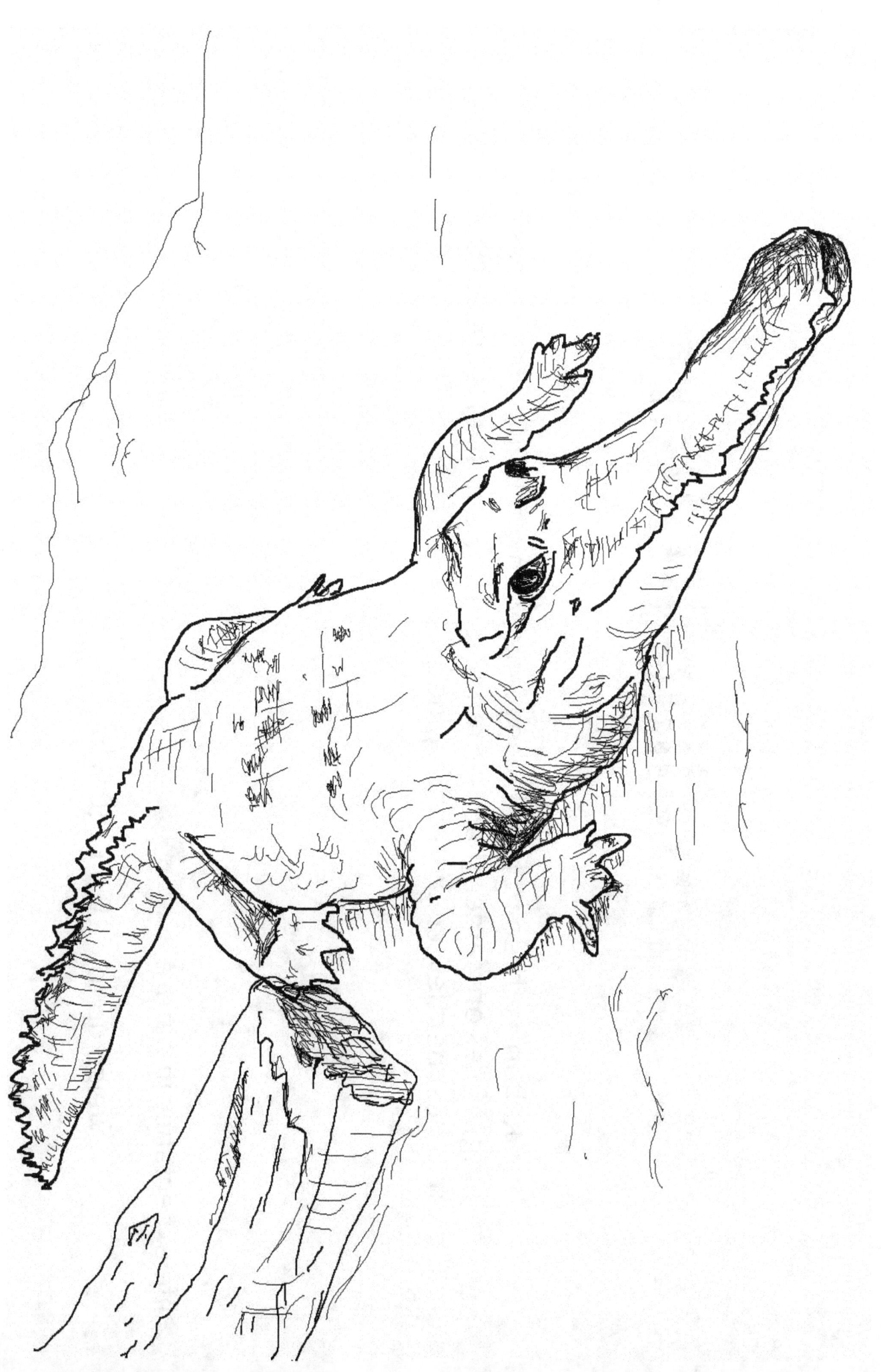

Australian Kultarr

The Kultarr is three to four inches long, with a tail up to ten inches long. Males are larger than the females. They eat invertebrates like roaches, beetles, crickets and spiders.

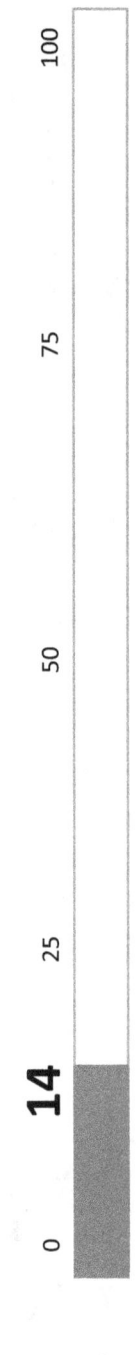

life expectancy in nature

0   **14**   25   50   75   100

weigh up to   0,4 kg (0,8 lb)

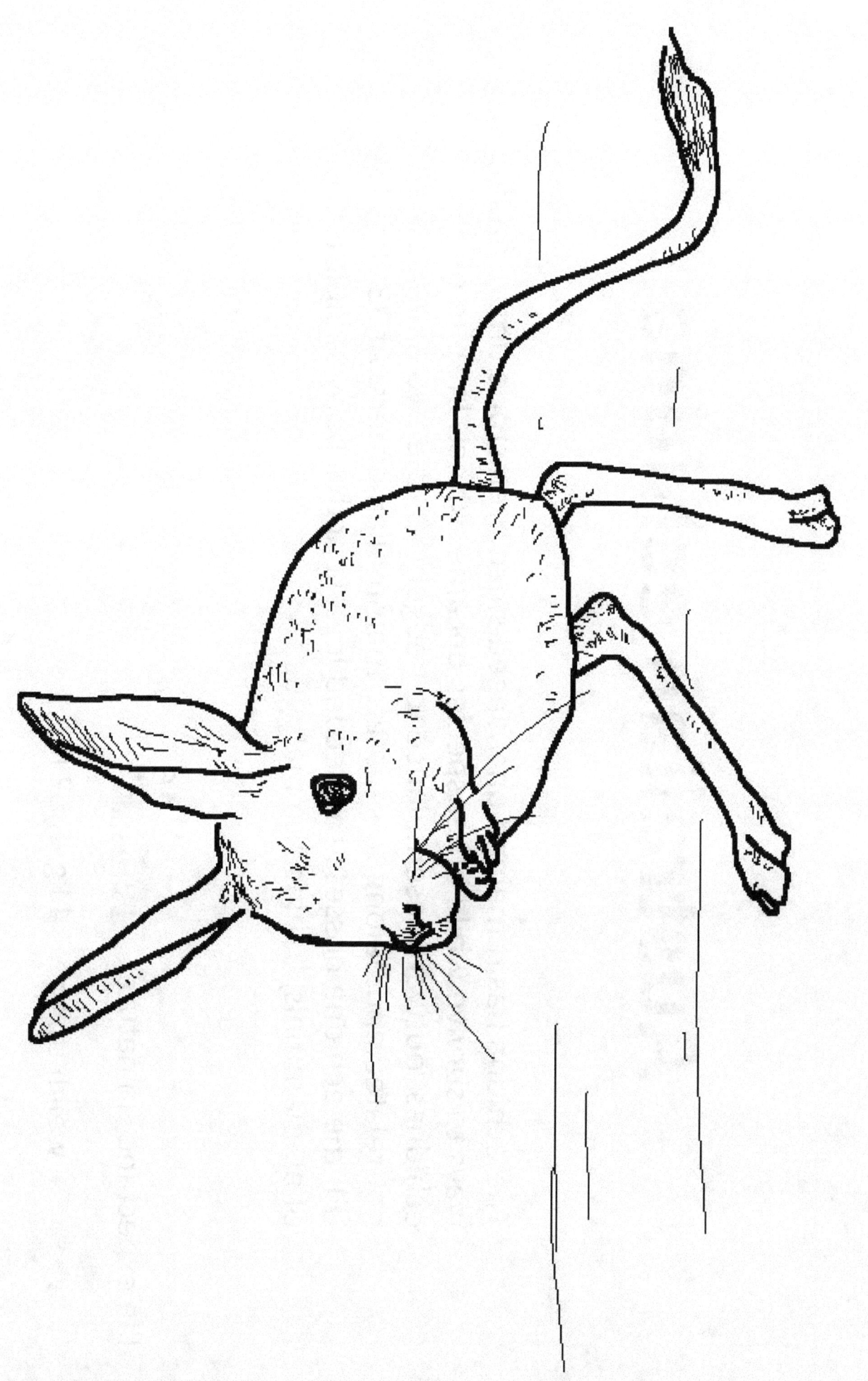

Australian echidna

The echidna has remained unchanged since prehistoric times, finding ways to survive while other species became extinct. In spite of echidnas' outward resemblance to hedgehogs, the two animals are not related and belong to separate mammalian orders. At 33 °C (91.4 °F), the echidna possess the second lowest active body temperature of all mammals, behind the platypus.

life expectancy in nature

| 0 | **16** | 25 | 50 | 75 | 100 |

weigh up to   4 kg (8,82 lb)

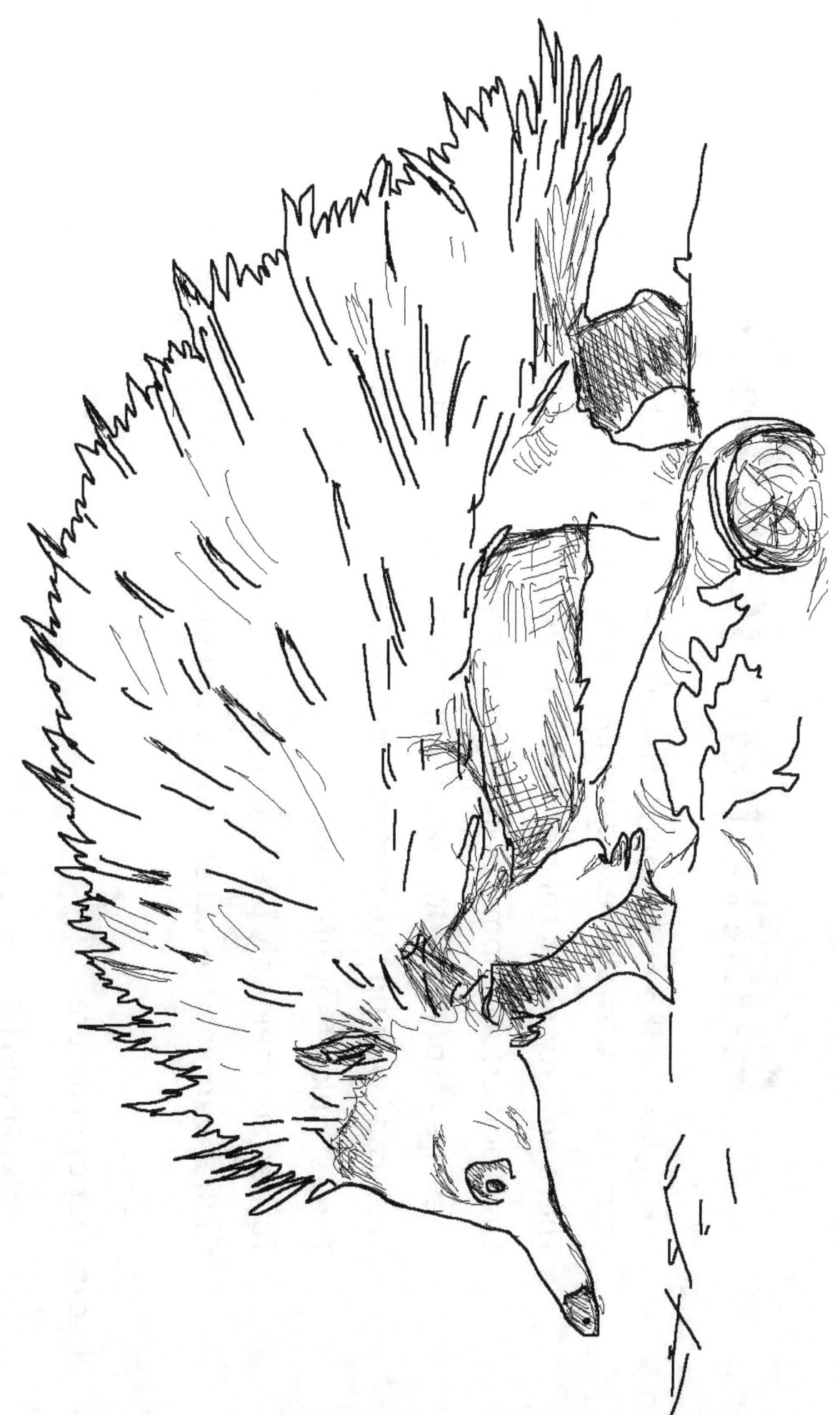

Australian jellyfish

Is considered the most venomous marine animal. So, before you plan your trip to Australia read carefully the following facts:

There are around 50 species of box jellyfish.

Their powerful venom lies in their tentacles.

They are responsible for over 60 deaths in the last 100 years.

They can swim up to 6 meters per minute.

They shrink if they don't eat.

Turtles are their only predators.

Global warming has caused them to spend more time in our waters.

life expectancy in nature

| 0 | 2 | 25 | 50 | 75 | 100 |

weigh up to   6 kg (13 lb)

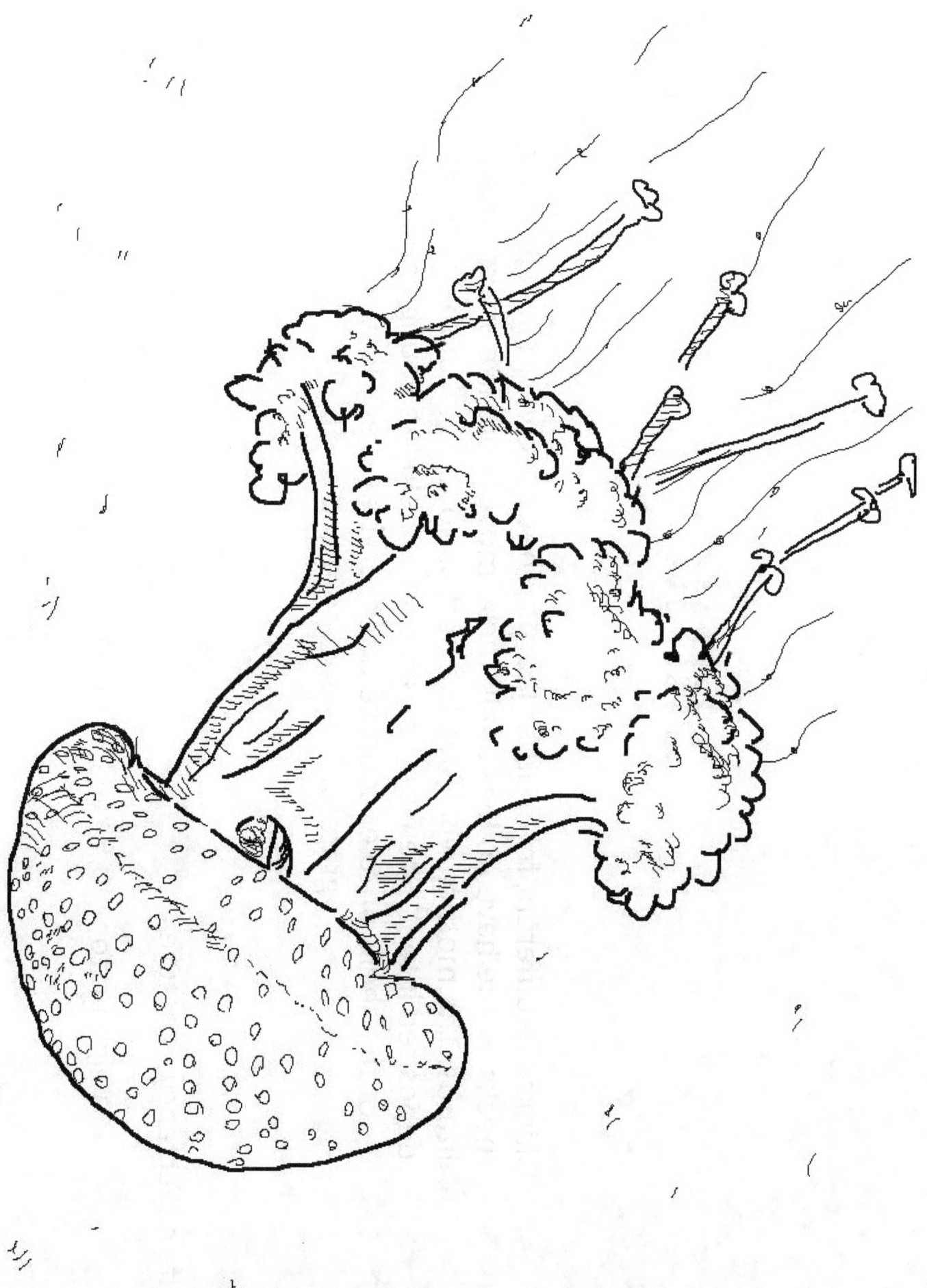

Skink

Skinks are different from other lizards. They have very small legs and necks. Some have no legs at all; these move more like snakes than lizards. The mother will leave the nest as soon as all of the eggs are deposited into it. She won't be around to help the young come out of the shells or to encourage their survival in any way. Yes, be grateful for your mom and dad!

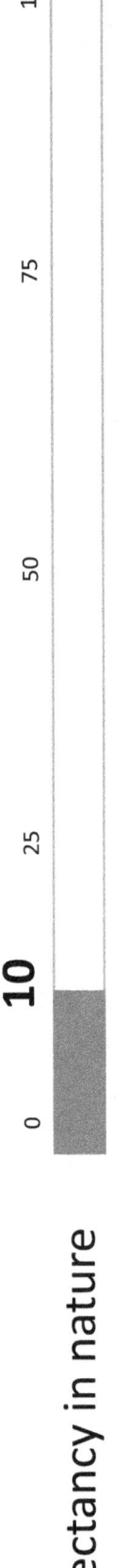

0   10   25   50   75   100

life expectancy in nature

weigh up to   0,5 kg (1,2 lb)

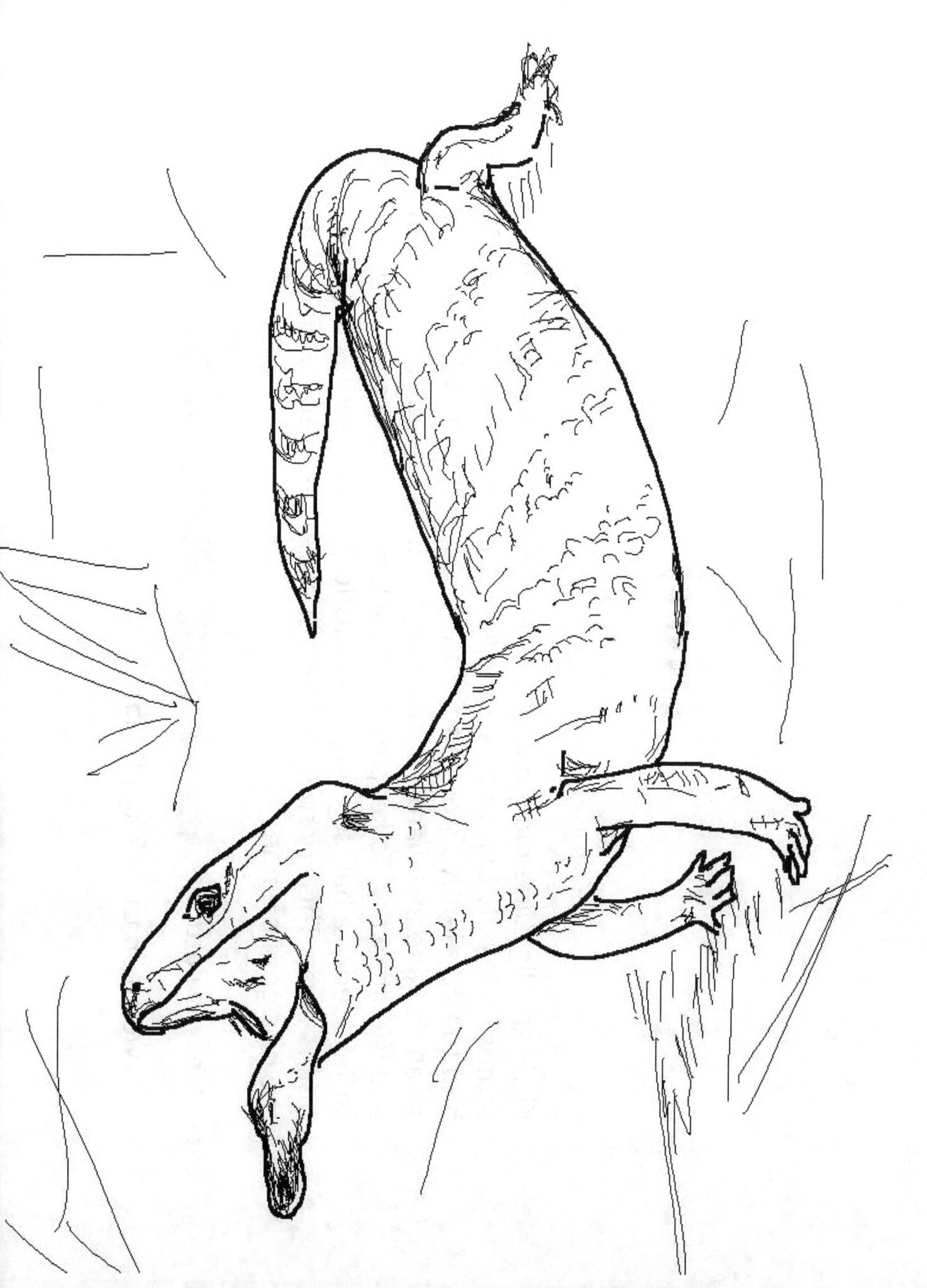

kiwi

Kiwis are flightless birds native to New Zealand. Four toes (other ratites have only two or three) on each thick foot allow the flightless bird to pad silently through the forest in search of food. Despite its small size and awkward appearance, the kiwi can outrun a human and is quite wary. To keep track of each other in the dark, kiwis can shriek loudly, a half scream, half whistle that also serves to scare others away. This cry sounds like "kee-wee, kee-wee," which is how the bird got its name.

life expectancy in nature

0   25   50   **60**   75   100

weigh up to   2 kg (4,2 lb)

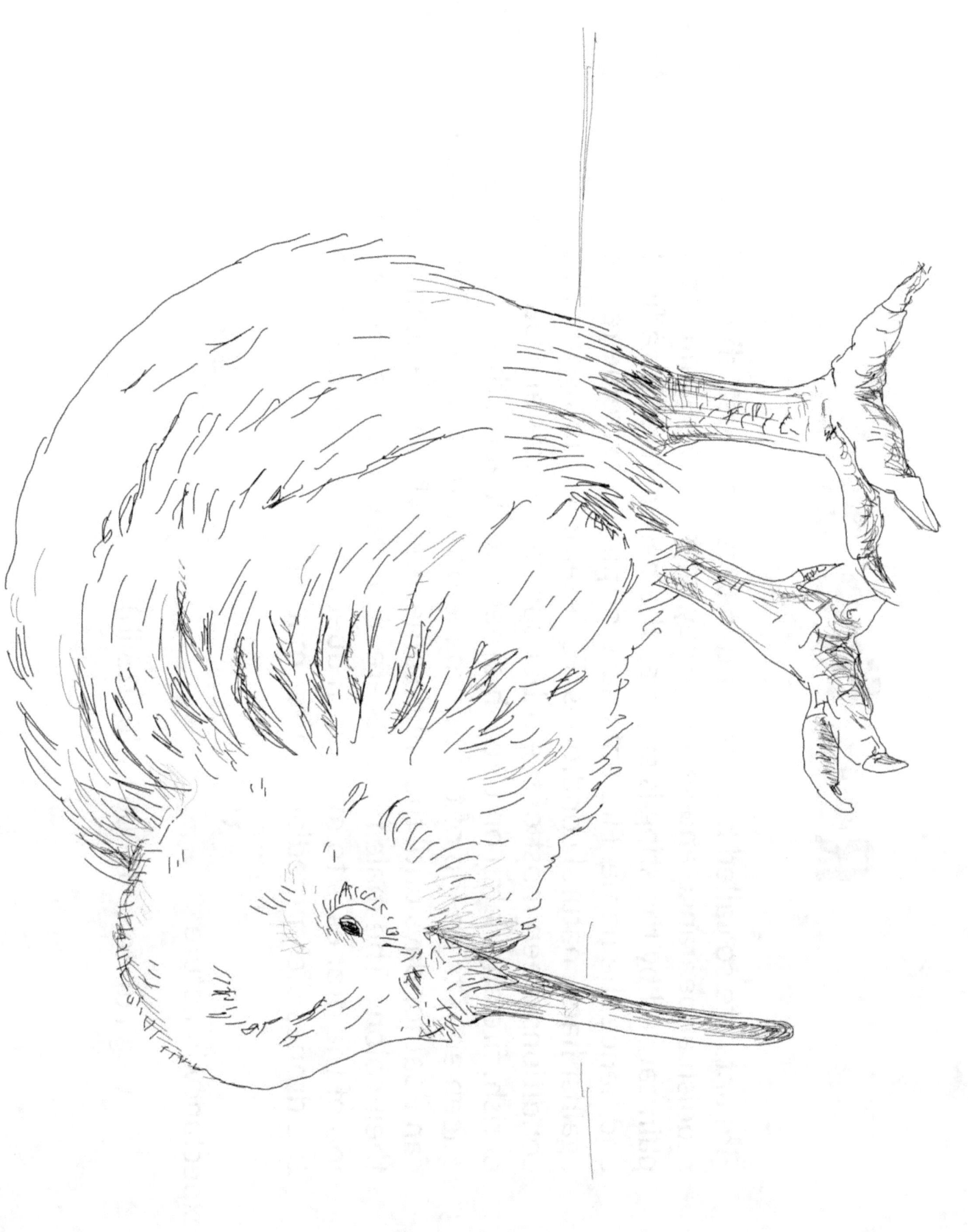

Red fire ant

Fire ants are so called because of two reasons – first, they have a reddish appearance and second, they have a very painful sting. The pain caused by the sting is same as the pain caused by a fire burn and hence the name. Fire ants have displayed extreme resilience against harsh natural conditions. For example, during flooded conditions when most of the other species of ants and other insects perish, fire ants latch on to each other and float on the water. The queen ant sits on top of the raft made up of worker ants. The ant raft can float for days until they find some land where they can create their colony. The male fire ants are also known as the drones. The job of the drones is to mate with queen ants. Interestingly however, the drones die immediately after mating.

life expectancy in nature

0   **3**   25   50   75   100

weigh up to   0,006 kg (0,013 lb)

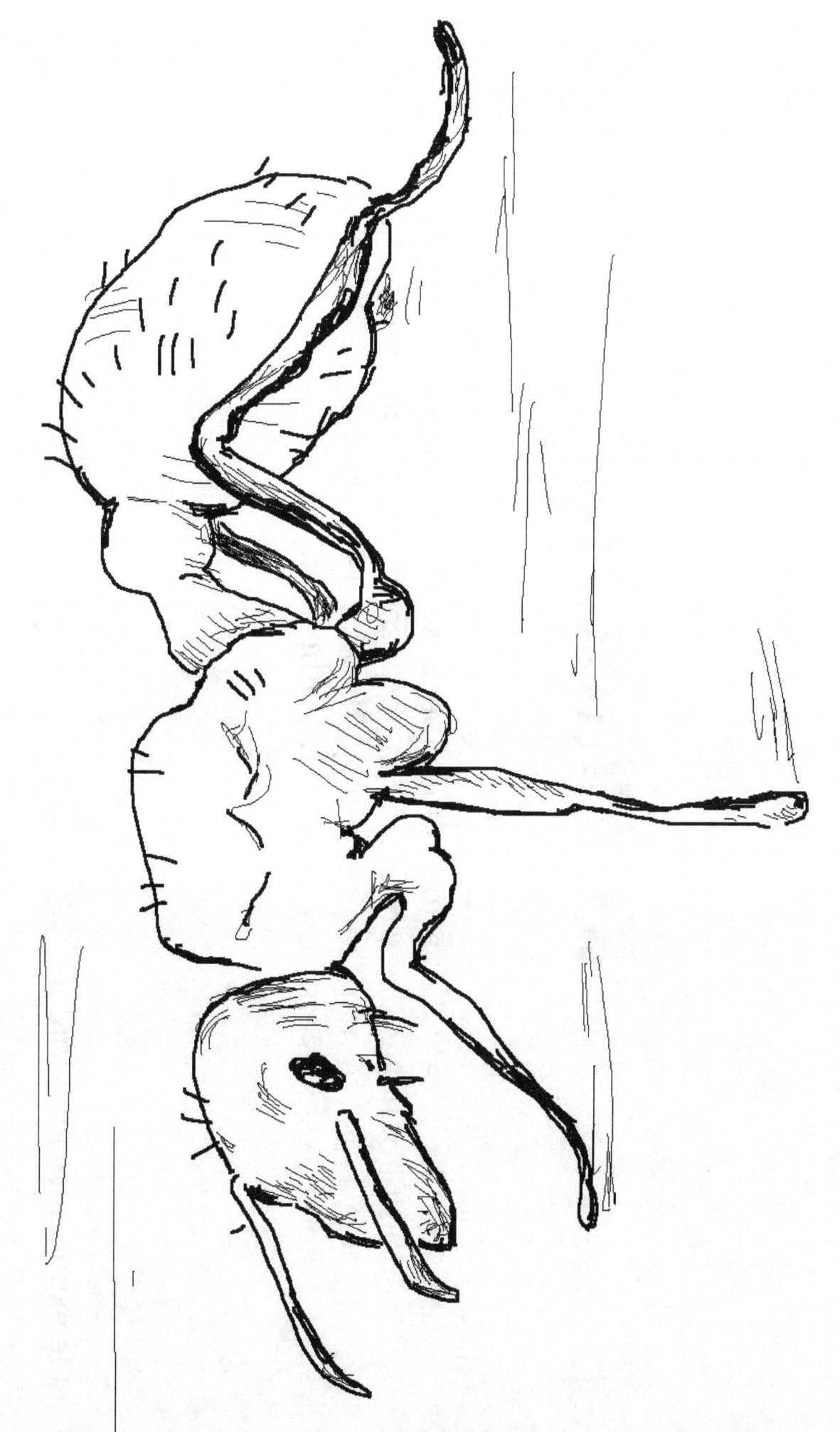

Kookaburra

The bird is called as a kookaburra because of the laughing call that this bird makes. They don't laugh because they see something funny, they laugh to mark their territory. They lay 1-5 eggs in a tree hollow and the chicks are born blind and featherless.

life expectancy in nature

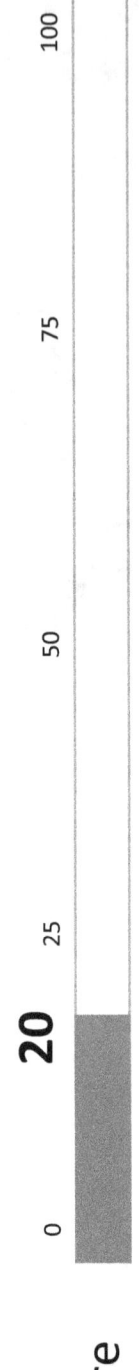

0   20   25   50   75   100

weigh up to   0,5 kg (1,1 lb)

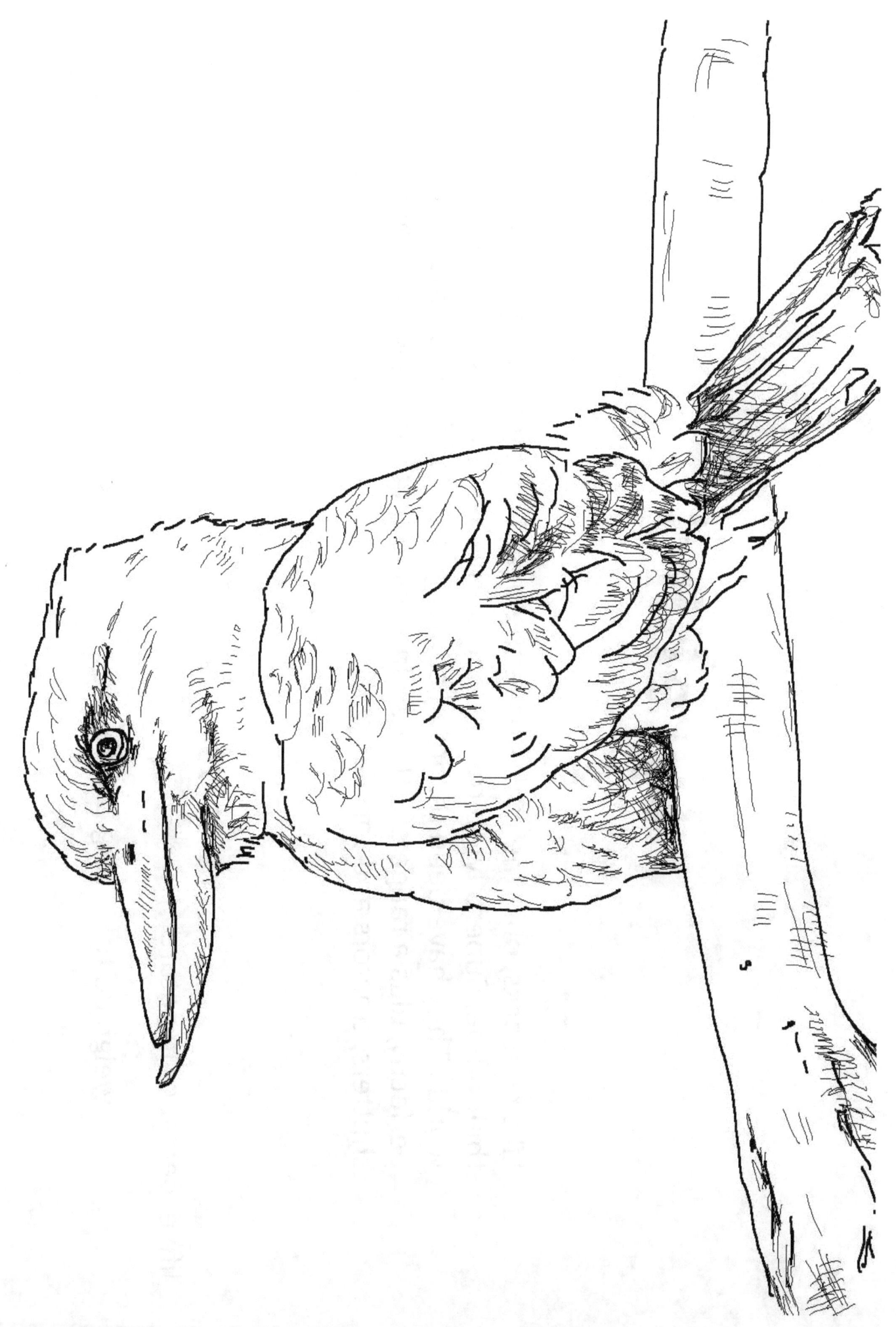

Lyrebird

Like peacocks, only the males have the beautiful tails that give them their name. Superb lyrebirds are one of the best mimics in the bird world. They have been recorded copying other bird and animal calls perfectly, plus a range of other sounds including chainsaws, camera shutters, tractors and car alarms.

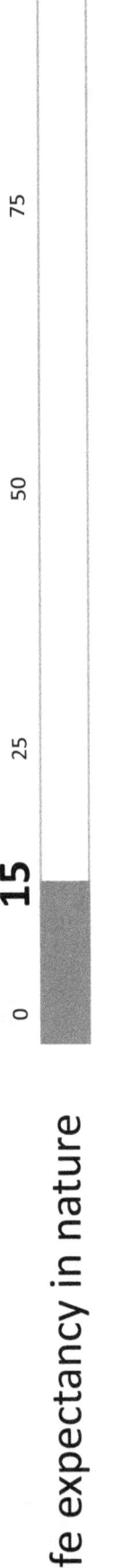

life expectancy in nature

weigh up to   1 kg (2,3 lb)

0   **15**   25   50   75   100

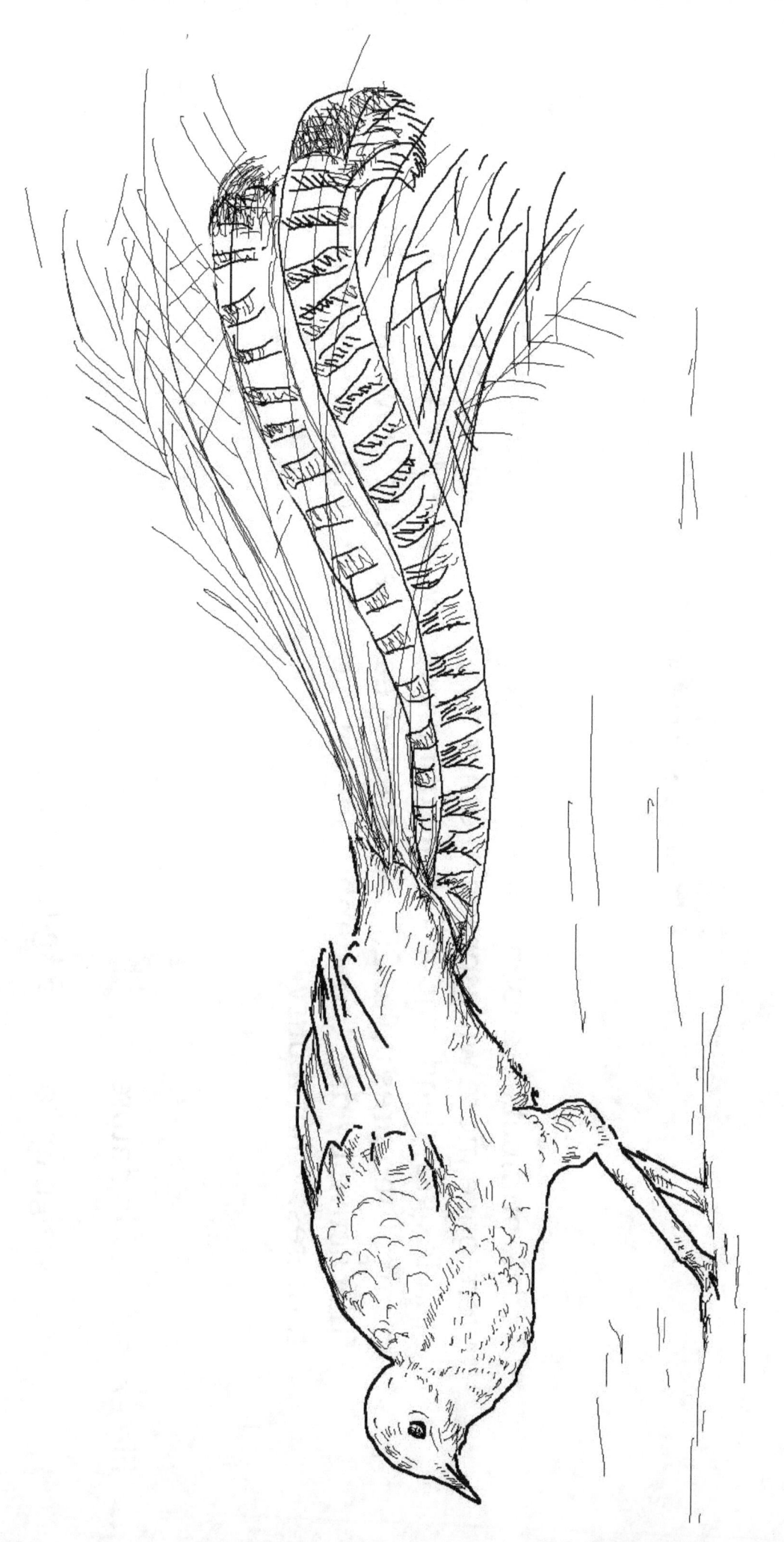

Numbat

Today, numbats are found only in areas of eucalypt forest, but they were once more widespread in other types of semiarid woodland, spinifex grassland, and in terrain dominated by sand dune. An adult numbat requires up to 20,000 termites each day. The only marsupial fully active by day, the numbat spends most of its time searching for termites. What a busy life!

life expectancy in nature

0   **5**   25   50   75   100

weigh up to   0.5 kg (1.2 lb)

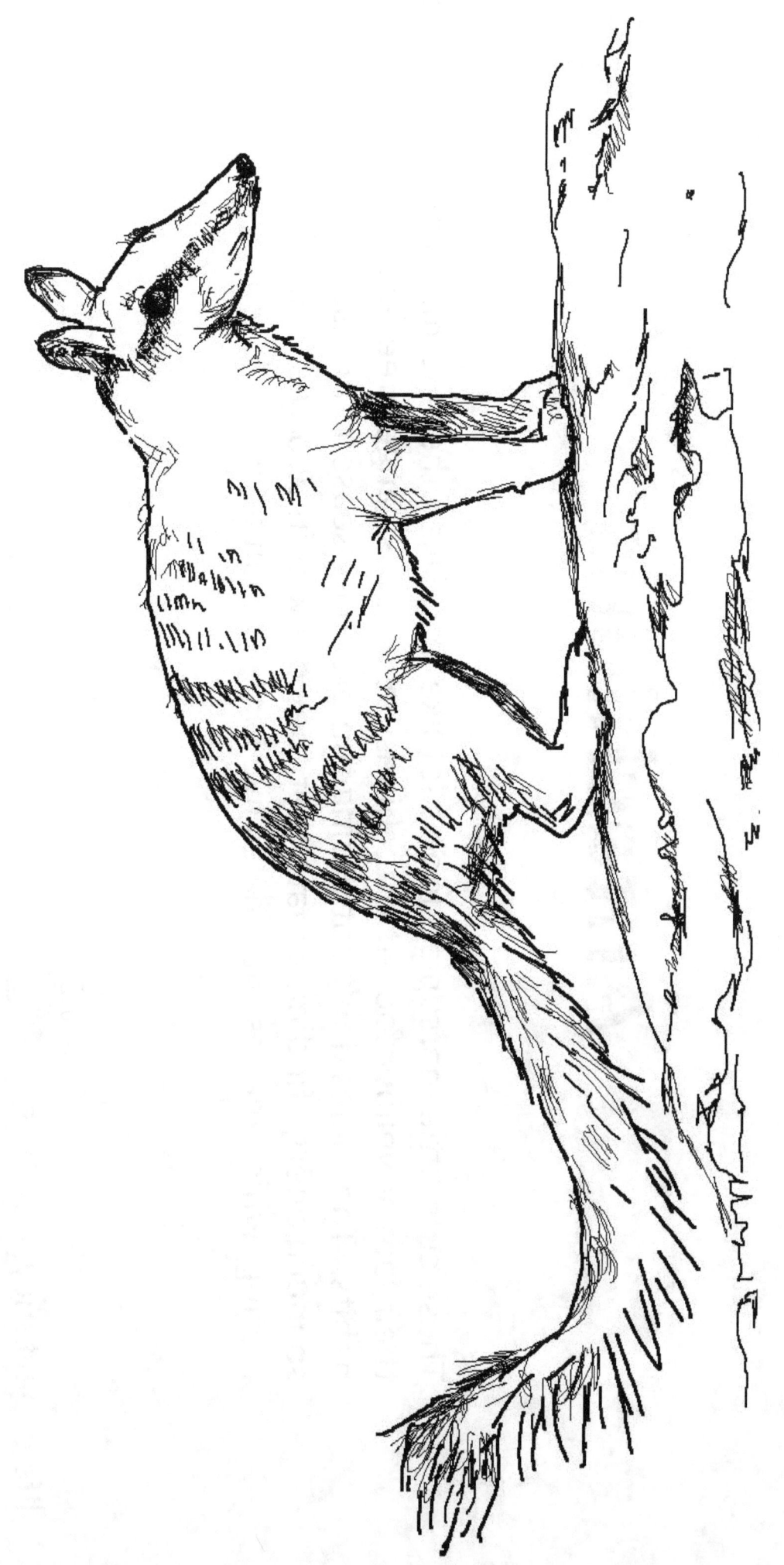

Antechinus

These cute little marsupials look a lot like rats. Like other members of their family, yellow-footed antechinus have very strange breeding habits. The males don't eat during the breeding season and use up so much energy finding a mate that they die within two weeks of mating, which means that males live for less than a year.

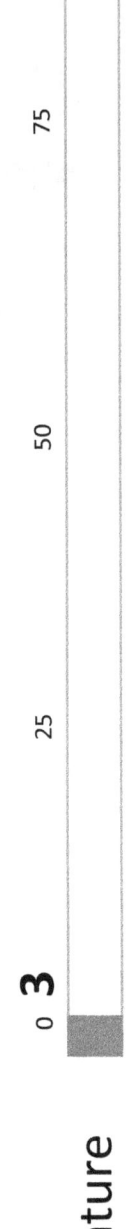

0   25   50   75   100

3

life expectancy in nature

weigh up to   0,3 kg (0,65 lb)

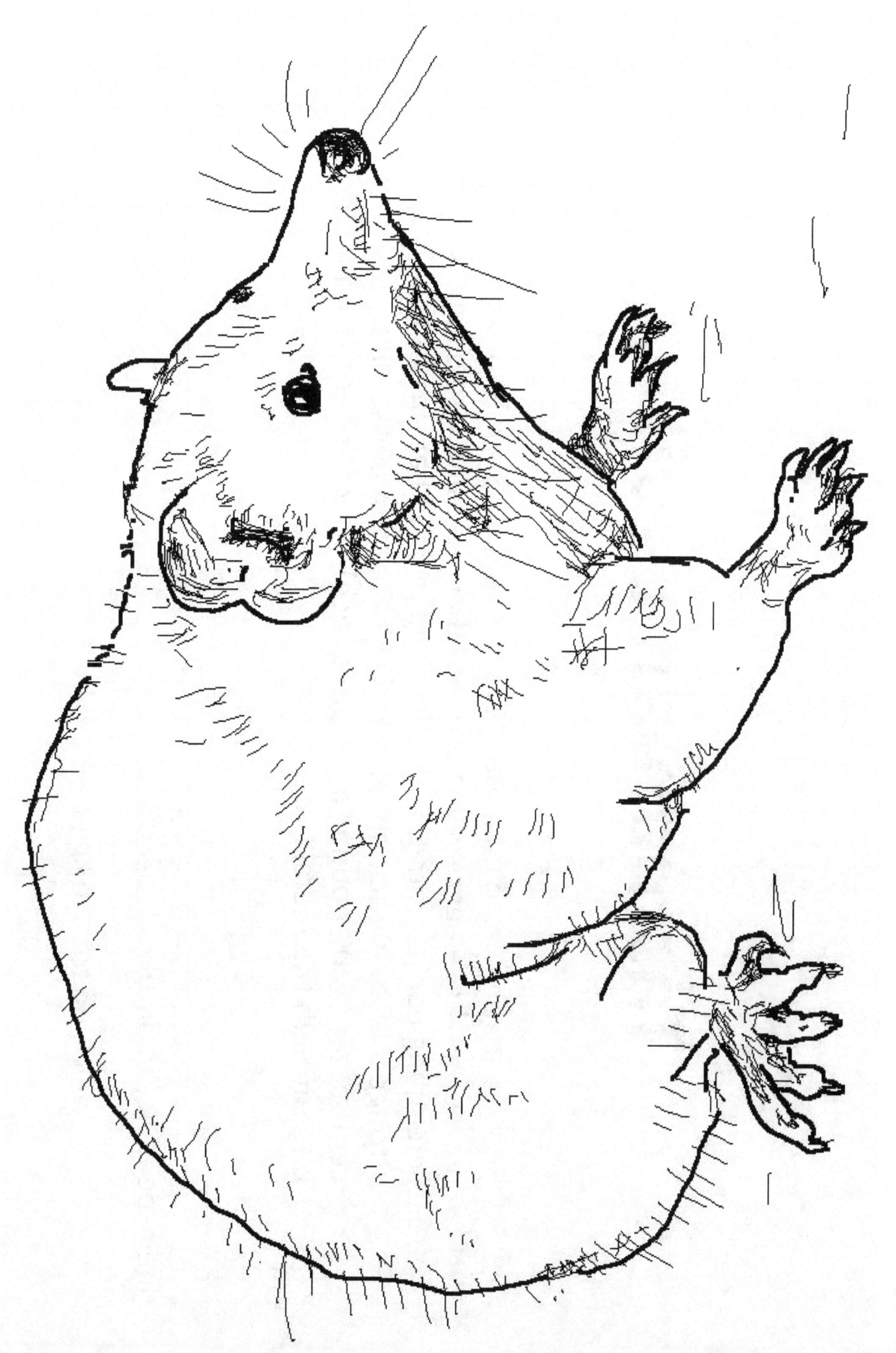

Tasmanian devil

The fascinating Tasmanian devil is a carnivorous, semi-nocturnal creature, whose aggressive nature and wild hissing, growling and screaming earned it the name. Tasmanian devil has one of the strongest bites in the animal world; 84 kilogram per square centimeter (1200 pounds per square inch), which means that it can bite through the metal trap.

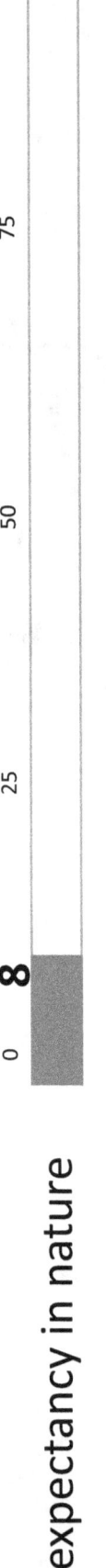

life expectancy in nature

weigh up to   6 kg (13,2 lb)

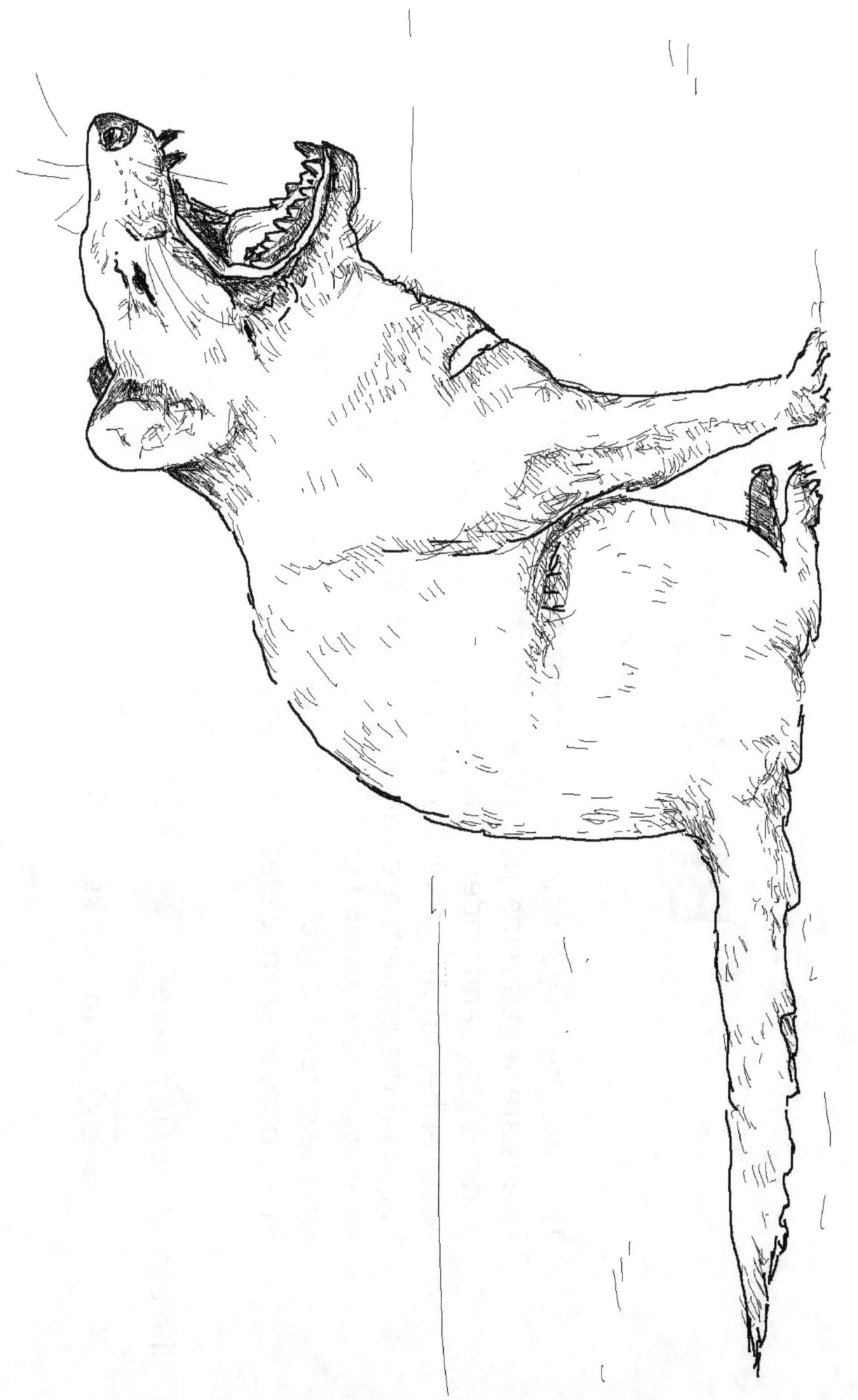

Black Swan

They are the only species of swan that is completely black. Black swans are vegetarians, using their meter-long necks to reach down and eat algae and underwater weeds. They mate for life and build nests either on the ground or floating on the water. They lay 4-6 eggs and the cygnets are very cute and fluffy. The mum and dad are very aggressive around their babies and will protect them fiercely. On the ground, a group of black swans is called a bank. When flying in a group, they are called a wedge.

20

| 0 | 25 | 50 | 75 | 100 |

life expectancy in nature

weigh up to   8 kg (17,6 lb)

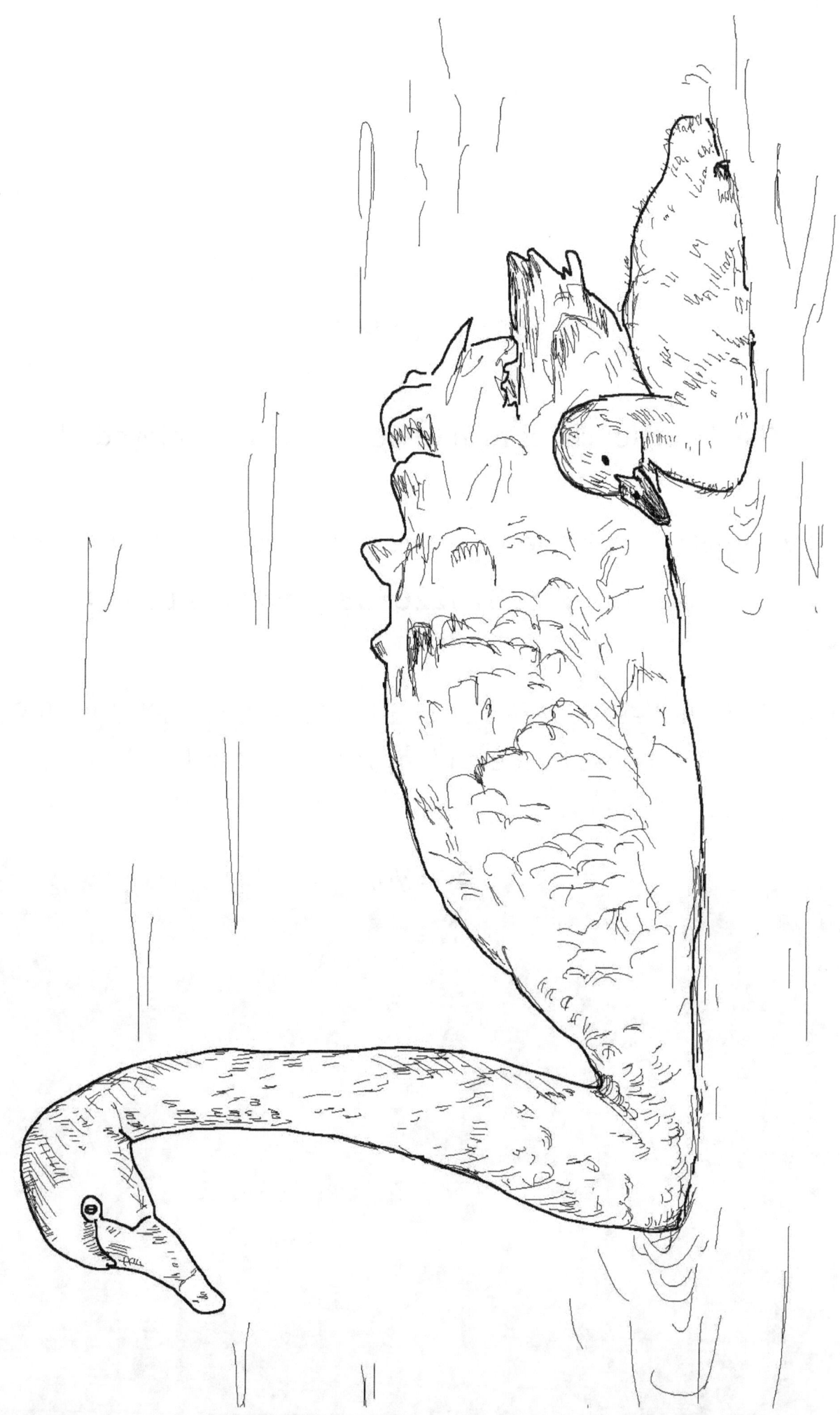

Dear Reader!

Thank you for choosing my book! Hope you enjoyed it!

If you really liked it, please, **leave a short review on Amazon!**
Use ISBN # 9781079226393 to find this book

Check out my website http://21centurywritersclub.com/ for more
books by me and my fellow writers!

See ya,
Mark

SEARCH MORE COLORING BOOKS

Book Series: Animal Planet

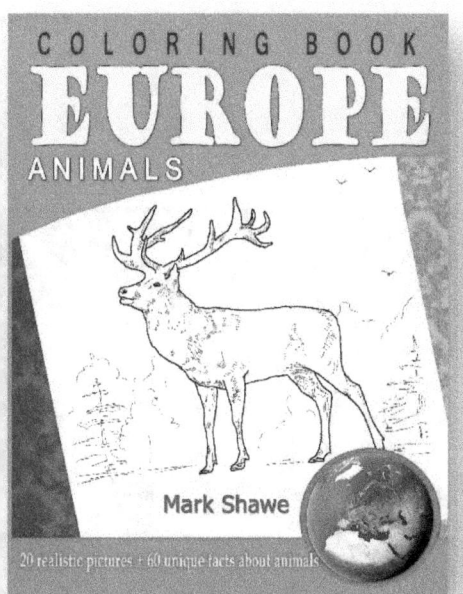

Animals of Europe

ISBN # 9781079222258

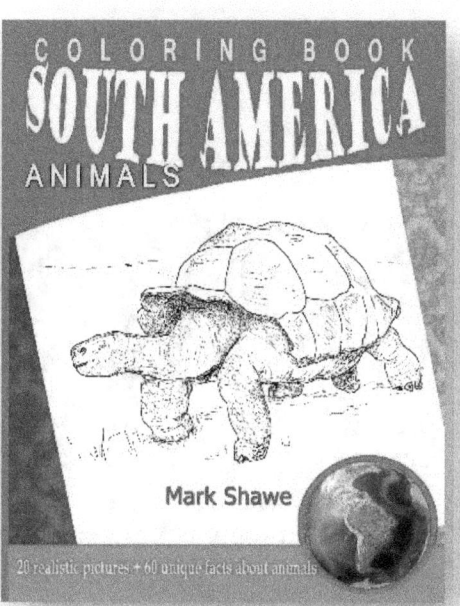

Animals of South America

ISBN # 9781079222920

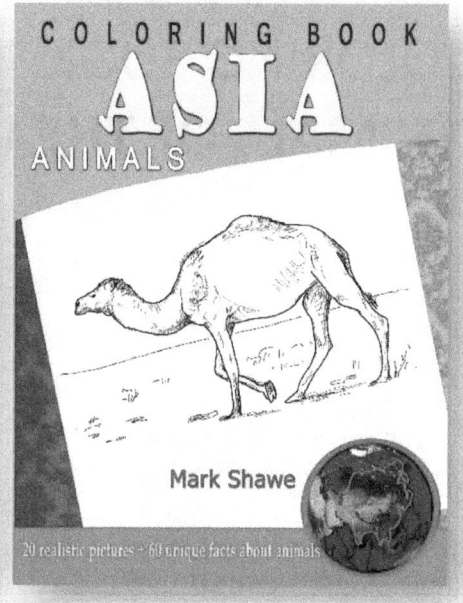

Animals of Asia

ISBN # 9781079224740

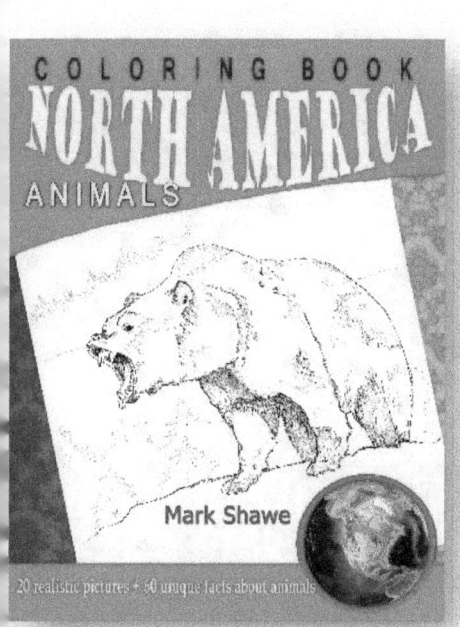

Animals of North America

ISBN # 9781079225525

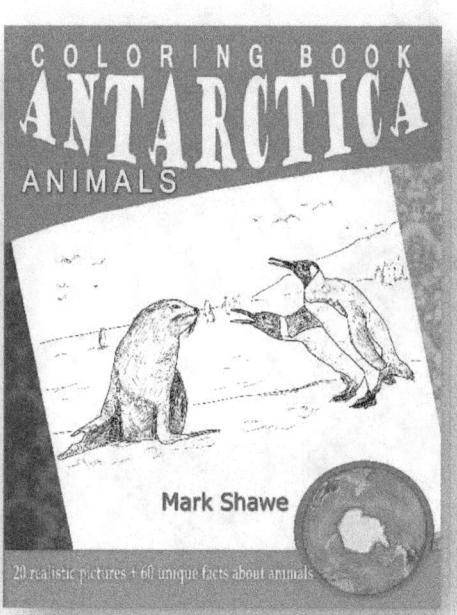

Animals of Antarctica

ISBN # 9781079225969

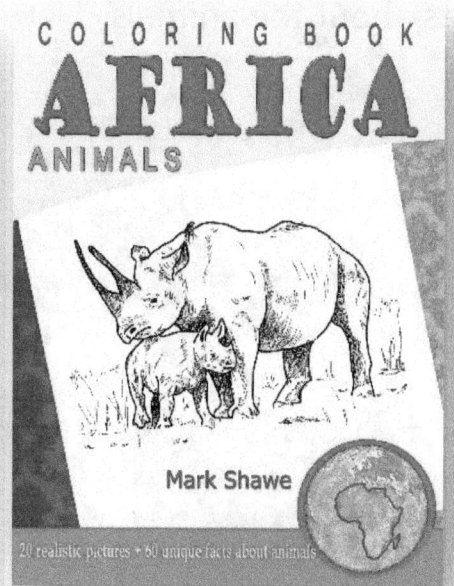

Animals of Africa

ISBN # 9781079227536

SPECIAL EDITION

COLORING BOOK:

ANIMALS OF THE WORLD

140 original realistic full-page images of wild animals of the World on single-sided sheets to prevent bleed-through

420 interesting unusual facts about the animals

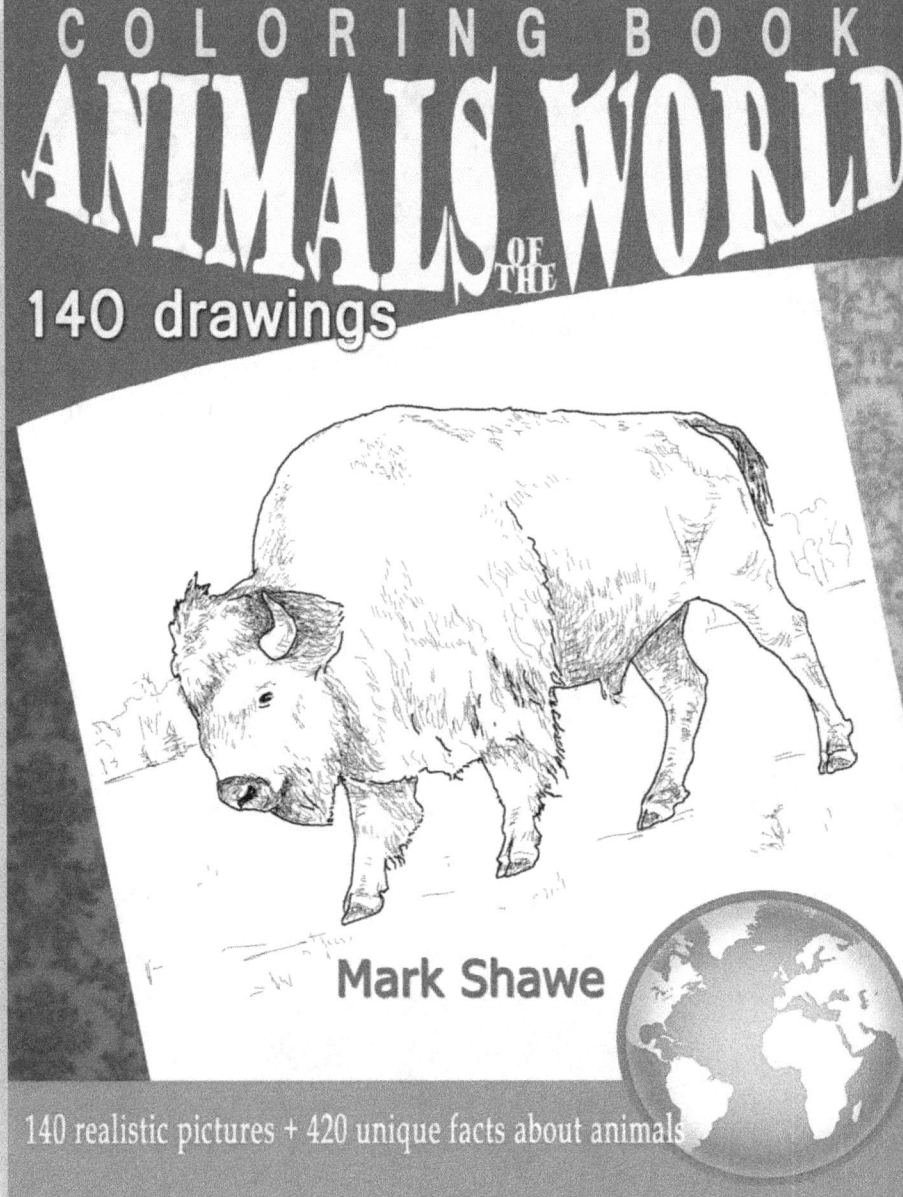

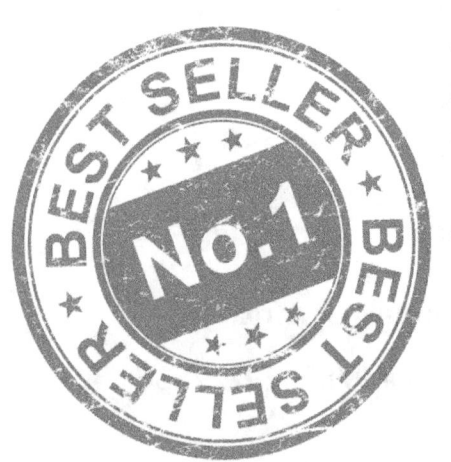

ISBN # 9781079226799

Book Series: **Animal Planet**

www.ingramcontent.com/pod-product-compliance
Lightning Source LLC
Chambersburg PA
CBHW081020170526

45158CB00010B/3116